Pinching Crayfish

by Janet Piehl

PULL AHEAD BOOKS

Animals

Lerner Publications Company • Minneapolis

For Elsworth Rockefeller
Special thanks to Francis M. Veraldi

Text copyright © 2008 by Janet Piehl
Illustrations copyright © Laura Westlund/Independent Picture
Service, pp. 28, 29.

Lerner Publications Company
A division of Lerner Publishing Group, Inc.
241 First Avenue North
Minneapolis, MN 55401 U.S.A.

Website address: www.lernerbooks.com

Words in *italic* type are explained in a glossary on page 30.

Library of Congress Cataloging-in-Publication Data

Piehl, Janet.
    Pinching crayfish / by Janet Piehl.
        p.   cm. — (Pull ahead books)
    Includes index.
    ISBN-13: 978–0–8225–5931–3 (lib. bdg. : alk. paper)
    1. Crayfish—Juvenile literature. I. Title.
    QL444.M33P54 2008
    595.3'84—dc22   2006028870

Manufactured in the United States of America
1 2 3 4 5 6 — JR — 13 12 11 10 09 08

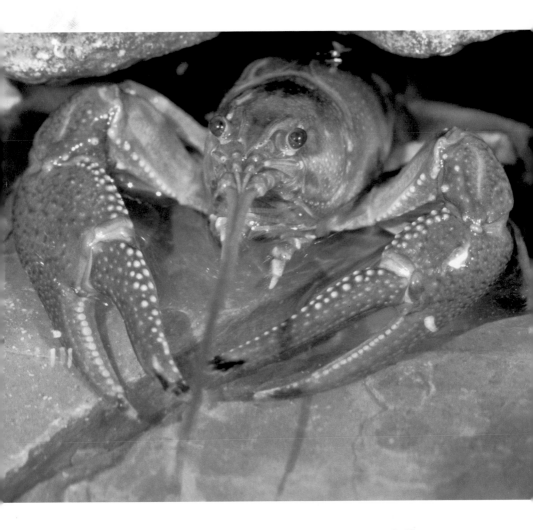

What is hiding under that rock?

It is waving two big claws.

It is a crayfish. Crayfish hide under rocks or logs during the day. They come out at night.

Crayfish live in lakes, rivers, streams, and swamps. Have you seen crayfish near your home?

Behind a crayfish's claws are eight legs. A crayfish crawls on land and in the water with its legs.

A crayfish has *swimmerets* on its underside. They look like small legs.

Swimmerets help a crayfish swim. A crayfish uses its tail to swim too.

A crayfish sees with two eyes. They are on short stalks on its head. The stalks can move even when the rest of the crayfish is still.

Antennas help a crayfish feel, taste, and smell.

A crayfish has two short antennas and two long antennas on its head.

A crayfish has a tough shell. The
shell is called an *exoskeleton*. Is a
crayfish a fish?

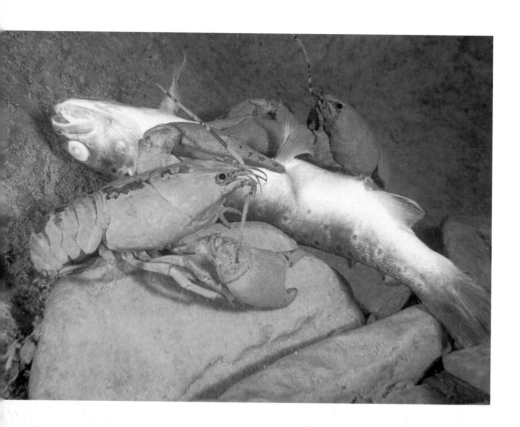

No. A crayfish is a *crustacean*.
Crustaceans have exoskeletons and
two pairs of antennas. Fish do not
have exoskeletons or antennas.

A crayfish's exoskeleton makes it hard for enemies to hurt it. A crayfish can wave its claws when it sees an enemy.

Sometimes an enemy comes too close. A crayfish attacks it by pinching the enemy with its claws.

Claws also help a crayfish find food.
It searches for food using its claws,
eyes, and antennas.

Crayfish eat snails, fish, worms, and plants that live in water. Crayfish also eat dead plants and animals.

Snap! This crayfish catches a fish with its claws.

Crayfish are
food for
other
animals.

Alligators, fish, birds, raccoons, and turtles hunt and eat crayfish.
People eat crayfish too.

How are crayfish born? A female crayfish lays eggs in the spring. They stick to the mother's swimmerets. The eggs look like berries.

Baby crayfish hatch from the eggs after a few weeks. The babies look like tiny adult crayfish. They are attached to their mother.

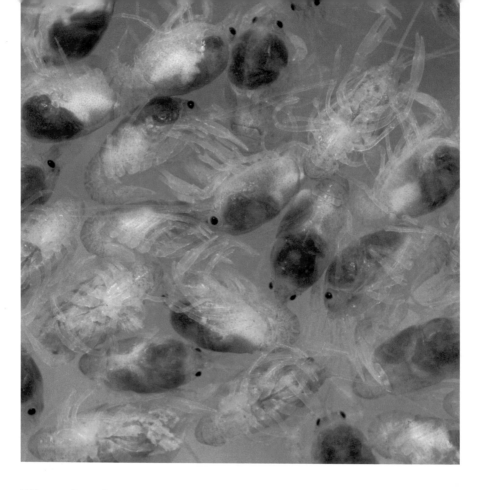

The babies have exoskeletons.
Their bodies are growing quickly.
But their exoskeletons do not grow.

The young crayfish shed their exoskeletons. This is called *molting*. They have grown new exoskeletons.

Soon the young crayfish are no longer attached to their mother. But they stay near her.

The young crayfish grow and grow.
They molt again. Then they leave
their mother.

The young crayfish look for food
and watch for enemies.

They wave and snap their claws.
They hide under rocks and logs.

Have you
ever found
a crayfish?
Be careful if
you pick
one up.
You could
get pinched!

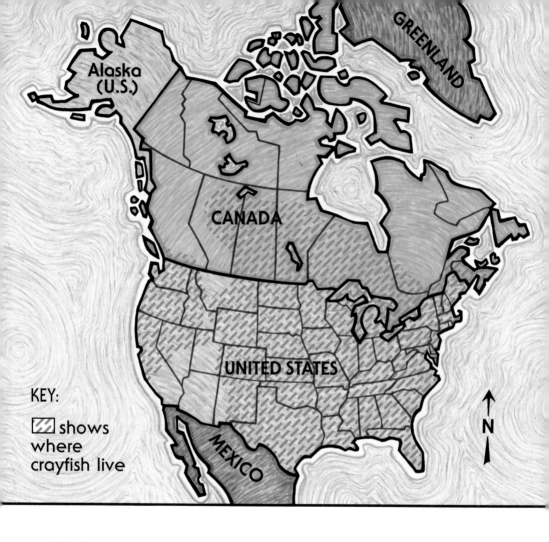

KEY:

🔲 shows where crayfish live

Alaska (U.S.)

GREENLAND

CANADA

UNITED STATES

MEXICO

N

Find your state or province on this map.
Do crayfish live near you?

Parts of a Crayfish's Body

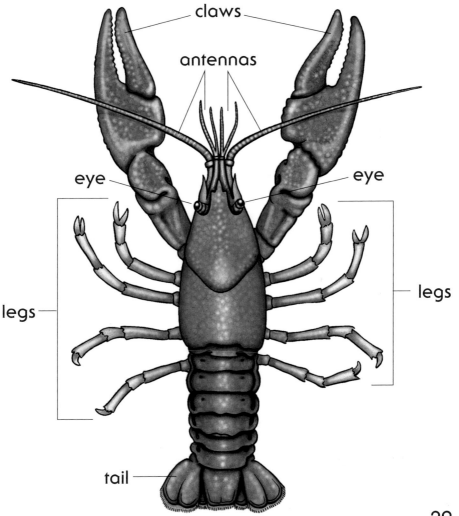

claws

antennas

eye

eye

legs

legs

tail

Glossary

antennas: thin feelers on a crayfish's head. Crayfish use antennas to feel, taste, and smell. Crayfish have four antennas.

crustacean: a kind of animal with a hard shell and two pairs of antennas. Crayfish, crabs, lobsters, and shrimp are crustaceans.

exoskeleton: the hard covering or shell of a crayfish

molting: outgrowing and shedding an outer covering. A crayfish sheds its old shell. Then a new shell hardens.

swimmerets: small, leglike body parts on the underside of a crayfish. They help a crayfish move. Female crayfish carry eggs on their swimmerets.

Further Reading and Websites

Crustacean Printouts
  http://www.enchantedlearning.com/subjects/
  invertebrates/crustacean/index.shtml

Freshwater Crayfish Album
  http://iz.carnegiemnh.org/crayfish/phpbb2/album
  _cat.php?cat_id=1

Grimm, Phyllis W. *Crayfish*. Minneapolis: Lerner
  Publications Company, 2001.

Morgan, Sally. *Crabs and Crustaceans*. North Mankato,
  MN: Thameside Press, 2001.

Sill, Cathryn. *About Crustaceans: A Guide for Children*.
  Atlanta: Peachtree Publishers, 2004.

Index

Photo Acknowledgments

The images in this book are used with the permission of: © Gary Meszaros/Visuals Unlimited, front cover, p. 22; © Steve Maslowski/Visuals Unlimited, p. 3; © Joe McDonald/CORBIS, p. 4; © Jerry Boucher, pp. 5, 8, 9, 10, 14, 20, 23, 24, 26; © age fotostock/SuperStock, p. 6; © Barry Mansell/naturepl.com, pp. 7, 11; © Fabio Liverani/naturepl.com, p. 12; © Gary Bell/zefa/Corbis, p. 13; © Breck P. Kent, pp. 15, 16, 21; © Daniel W. Gotshall/Visuals Unlimited, p. 17; © Ed Reschke/Peter Arnold, Inc., p. 18; © C. C. Lockwood/Animals Animals, p. 19; © Patrice Ceisel/Visuals Unlimited, p. 25; © Dwight R. Kuhn, p. 27.

Illustrations on pp. 28, 29 © Laura Westlund/Independent Picture Service.